Catherine Carey
in a Nutshell

Catherine Carey in a Nutshell

Copyright © 2015
MadeGlobal Publishing

ISBN-13: 978-84-944574-0-1

All rights reserved. No part of this publication may be reproduced, stored in a retrieval system, or transmitted, in any form or by any means, electronic, mechanical, photocopying, recording or otherwise, except as permitted by the UK Copyright, Designs and Patents Act 1988, without the prior permission of the publisher.

M
MadeGlobal Publishing

For more information on
MadeGlobal Publishing, visit our website:
www.madeglobal.com

For my grandmother, Dorothy Loy Swartz…
"Read a Book"

Cover: Catherine Carey Line Drawing by
Mohammad Rusdianto © 2015 MadeGlobal Publishing

Contents

Introduction 3
Birth and paternity 7
Early childhood 19
Courtship and marriage 23
Children 35
Catherine at Henry VIII's court 47
Exile 57
Catherine and Henry 65
Catherine at Elizabeth I's court 71
Death 75
Acknowledgements 81

Catherine Carey's Family Tree Through Mary Boleyn

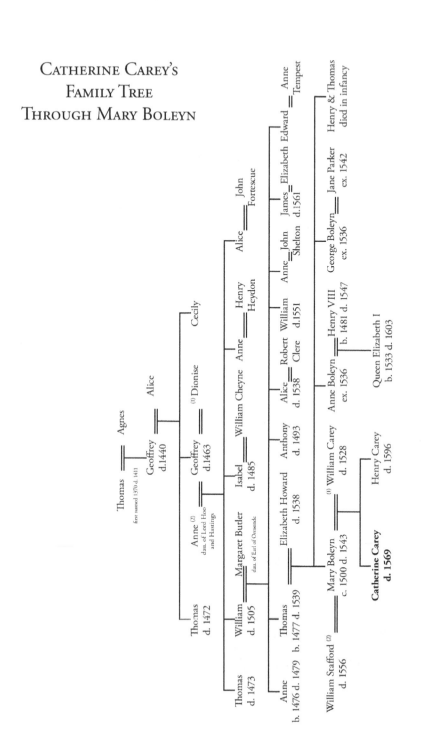

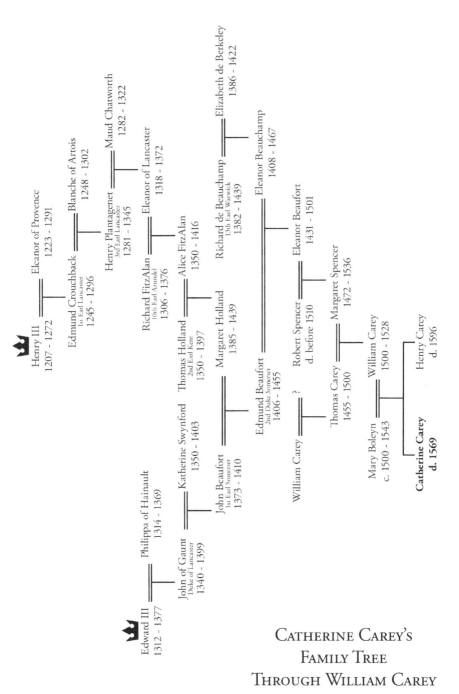

CATHERINE CAREY'S
FAMILY TREE
THROUGH WILLIAM CAREY

Introduction

An Associate Conservator of Paintings for the Yale Center for British Art in New Haven, Connecticut, has spent the last three years meticulously examining the portrait of a woman painted over 450 years ago. The woman in the painting has undergone some cosmetic improvements over the years – her true features hidden under a few layers of paint and varnish. Her fair skin now looks slightly orange, the crinkles around her eyes have been airbrushed away. The deterioration is significant enough that a conservation effort has been started to return the painting to its original glory and reveal the true face of the woman it honours.

The restoration being carried out on the *Portrait of a Woman, probably Catherine Carey, Lady Knollys* by Steven Van der Meulen is so poignant because Catherine's history, just like her painted face, has become hidden over time. It is only recently that she has joined the spotlight that has been shining for years on her other Tudor brethren.

HISTORY "In a Nutshell" SERIES

Figure 1 - Portrait of a woman,
probably Catherine Carey, Lady Knollys
by Steven van der Meulen, 1562

Why has she been relatively ignored by historians for the better part of five centuries? In the last four years of researching her, I have found few secondary resources analysing anything beyond the paternity of this incredible Tudor woman. Catherine was more than just the possible illegitimate daughter of Henry VIII. She was a mother, a sister and a wife. She was a religious reformer, a trusted confidante and a loyal friend. It is time to finally bring Catherine's story out of the darkness and into the light.

Catherine Carey experienced much in her short life. She was born into a country on the brink of reformation to parents high in the favour of a charismatic and truculent king. A turbulent childhood commenced with the death of her accepted father, William Carey, of the dreaded sweating sickness on 22 June 1528, shortly into her fourth year. It was an event that put her mother's finances on unstable footing and, no doubt, changed the course of a future that had been carefully plotted out for her by her parents.

All the uncertainty that clouded Catherine's early days seemed to melt away the moment, almost exactly five years later, that her aunt, Anne Boleyn, was crowned Queen of England on 1 June 1533 in Westminster Abbey. The Boleyn family had reached their zenith. Anne was full with child and high in the king's graces. It was predicted that she carried the boy that Henry had so longed for. It was only logical that Anne's good fortune would extend to her family members. Catherine and her brother, Henry, were practically guaranteed to reap the benefits of a close relationship to the queen.

Sadly, the golden future that Catherine dreamed of was shattered only three years later. The dawn of her adolescence was baptised in the blood of her aunt and uncle. On 17 May 1536, Catherine's uncle, George Boleyn, was the first of five men to be executed on Tower Hill for treasonous relationships with the queen. Anne, herself, followed behind only two days later, the first Queen of England to be beheaded.

HISTORY "In a Nutshell" SERIES

When Catherine reappears in the historical record, it is in the service of Henry's fourth wife, Anne of Cleves. As 1539 was drawing to a close, she finally found her own place at the English Court and paved the way for a future generation of Boleyn women that would serve their monarch – the generation that would eventually serve the highest ranking Boleyn woman of them all, Queen Elizabeth.

That was only the beginning of Catherine's story. This young woman from Kent would go on to marry well and give birth to a throng of children who would build very successful careers of their own. Her husband, Frances Knollys, was active in the Protestant Reformation and instrumental in the foundation of exile communities set up on the continent during the reign of Mary Tudor. Upon her return to England after the death of Mary I, Catherine went on to become a close confidante of Elizabeth I.

Catherine Carey was really the epitome of a successful Tudor woman. She excelled at just about everything that was expected of her as a woman of the Tudor period. In addition to serving four different queens, she uprooted her life to support her husband in his religious pursuits and managed to fill the Knollys cradle almost every other year for twenty-two years. Even more impressive, in an age of such a high infant mortality rate, only one out of fourteen births can be confirmed to have ended in an early death for the child.

The intent of this work is to give you a brief glimpse into the world that Catherine Carey inhabited and the life that she led. I hope you enjoy learning about her as much as I did and I am sure you will find that she was every bit as remarkable as the other Boleyn women who came before her.

Birth and paternity

It is fairly easy to pinpoint the birthdate of Henry, Catherine Carey's brother. Their father's inquisition post-mortem notes that his heir was aged two years, fifteen weeks, and five days on 22 June 1528[1] – pinpointing Henry's date of birth to 4 March 1526. Unfortunately, Catherine's exact date of birth is a bit murkier. As she was not William Carey's heir, she was not listed in the post-mortem. Making things more difficult is the fact that, in Tudor England, it was not considered common practice to record dates of birth unless, of course, the child was royal. Birthdates weren't even necessarily recorded if the child was of noble birth. Fortunately, we can estimate Catherine's entrance into the world based upon other circumstantial evidence.

The earliest mention Catherine receives is in the *Letters and Papers* of Henry VIII Volume XIV Part II. *Katharine Cary* is listed as a maid-of-honour to the king's new wife, Anne of Cleves.[2] While

1. Weir. Mary Boleyn pg 151
2. LP XIV Pt 2 572

HISTORY "In a Nutshell" SERIES

it was common at the time for younger children to serve and learn in households of the nobility, it was very uncommon for youths under the age of sixteen to serve an adult queen. A maid-of-honour position was not an opportunity for education – it required a young lady to already have the knowledge and skills required to serve a royal mistress. She should know card and dice games, have adequate sewing skills and familiarity with music and dance in order to entertain the queen. Interest and knowledge in the literary classics and mastery of multiple languages was also desirable. Only a few years prior, in 1537, Anne Bassett, the stepdaughter of Viscount Lisle, was rejected from a maid-of-honour post in Queen Jane Seymour's household because, at fifteen, she was considered too young. A year later, she was appointed to the coveted position.

The next mention of Catherine is in the parliament records of 1540. The parliament held in April ensured the ownership of the Knollys' manor at Rotherfield Greys in Oxfordshire to *Francis Knolles, Esq. and Katharine his wife* in the event of Francis's mother's death.[3] Based on these two records, it would be safe to assume that Catherine's marriage to Francis Knollys occurred some time between mid-November 1539 and mid-April 1540. The discovery of a Latin dictionary in a private collection of the Knollys' family by Sally Varlow seems to support this. An inscription on the inside cover in Francis' handwriting indicates:

> Here folowethe in order the names,
>   wt the tymes of the byrthe
> of the chyldren of Francys Knollys & Katern
>   his wyffe that
> were maryed ye xxvi daye of Aprylle anno. 1540.
> & the year of or Lorde is cownted to
>   begyne at krystmas.[4]

---

3. LP XV 498
4. Varlow pg 9

Birth and paternity

Regrettably, the date of Catherine's marriage is not enough evidence to settle her birth date. It was not unheard of for a marriage to occur very early in a child's life, particularly a child of noble birth. It was, however, very rare that those marriages were consummated before the age of sixteen. The same Latin dictionary includes a list of children born to Catherine and Francis. Their first child, Henry, was born the Tuesday before Easter Day in 1541.[5] This early conception proves that the marriage was not only consummated right away, but that Catherine and Francis were living as husband and wife.

The final piece of evidence for Catherine's birthdate is a portrait painted by the artist Steven Van der Meulen. It is dated 1562 and shows a heavily pregnant Elizabethan courtier in the final weeks of pregnancy. A contemporary inscription on the painting indicates that the sitter is in her thirty-eighth year. This painting was held in the collection of one of Catherine's descendants until its sale at Sotheby's[6] and has long been assumed to be a portrait of Catherine. The May 1562 date of birth listed in Francis's Latin dictionary for their final child, Dudley, supports this assumption. Furthermore, it narrows down the time of year for Catherine's birth to some time in the spring of 1524.

The date of Catherine's birth is an important piece of the puzzle in one of the most fiercely debated topics of Tudor history – the paternity of Mary Boleyn's children. While both Catherine and her brother, Henry, were given the last name of Mary's legal husband, some circumstantial evidence has cropped up to suggest that either one or both may have been fathered by Henry VIII.

Mary Boleyn's affair with the king has, over time, become accepted as common knowledge, but the reality is that there is only one piece of contemporary evidence to prove its occurrence. During the onset of the tumultuous debate that would come to be known

---

5. IBID
6. Weir, Mary Boleyn pg 160

HISTORY "In a Nutshell" SERIES

Figure 2 - William Carey (Catherine's father) attrib. Hans Holbein the Younger, circa 1528

as the King's Great Matter, a papal dispensation was issued by Pope Clement on 1 January 1528. This dispensation allowed that, should Henry's marriage to Catherine of Aragon be found null and void, he would be allowed to remarry any woman with whom he shared a first degree of affinity – namely, a woman who was the sister of a woman with whom he had illicit relations. At this time Henry was trying desperately to receive an annulment from Rome to marry Anne Boleyn so, though she is not specifically named, it is fairly certain that Mary is the sister the dispensation refers to.

Based upon the reference in the dispensation and the timeline of Henry's interest in Anne, the affair would have had to happen before 1526. As Henry Fitzroy, Henry's illegitimate child with Elizabeth Blount, was born in June 1519, it would be safe to assume that the relationship with Mary commenced during this period.

While it is possible that the affair began immediately after the birth of Fitzroy and before Mary's marriage to William Carey in February of 1520, Alison Weir in her biography on Mary Boleyn surmises that it happened after the marriage took place. She believes that the silver caparisons embroidered with the motto *Elle mon coeur a navera* (She has wounded my heart) that decorated the king's riding horse during the 2 March 1522 tournament in honour of the visiting ambassadors from Emperor Charles V, referred to Mary Boleyn.[7] Indeed, this would seem to coincide with the 4 February 1522 naming of Carey as keeper of the manor at Newhall and bailiff of the manors of Newhall, Boreham, Walkeforde Hall and Powers in Essex.[8]

A few months later, in May 1522, Carey and William West, a page of the chamber, were given the wardship of Thomas Sharpe, a man from Canterbury of limited mental capacity, and custody of his lands.[9] In April 1523, Carey is listed as a member of the

---

7. Weir, Mary Boleyn pg 118
8. L&P Vol III 2074 (5)
9. L&P Vol III 2297 (12)

Figure 3 - Portrait of Sir Francis Knollys (Catherine's husband), artist unknown

privy chamber and given an annuity of fifty marks[10] along with the receivership of the manor of Writtle. He is named bailiff and made keeper of Writtle Park in Essex.[11] Promotion to squire of the body and the keepership of Wanstead with 2*d* a day out of the issues of the manor along with three manors formerly belonging to the Duke of Buckingham,[12] followed in June 1524, mere months after the birth of Mary's first child, Catherine.

The final grants come in May 1526 – the keepership of the manor, garden and tower at Greenwich and rights to official lodgings there, and in June of the same year, the keepership of the parks of Ditton and Bucks with 3*d* a day.[13]

Is it possible that these grants were rewards for Carey's complicity in the king's affair with his wife? Could he have been given the manor of Wanstead to provide income for the care of the king's new-born illegitimate daughter? Certainly. However, William Carey was a treasured member of Henry's household and the king was known for treating his favourite courtiers well. In fact, the grants to Henry Norris, another close friend and servant, seem to mirror many of those same offices. In addition, William Carey was related to the royal family through the Beaufort line. As the king's cousin, it is only natural that he would receive generous offerings. As there are numerous possible reasons for the king's generosity towards William Carey, royal grants alone cannot be used as evidence that he fathered Carey's children.

There is a contemporary source that names Catherine's brother, Henry, as the illegitimate son of the king, but its source is questionable and, therefore, cannot be taken at face value. The country was in an uproar over the changes wrought by the king's reformation, which led to an uptick in rumour and gossip against

---

10. L&P Vol III 2993
11. L&P Vol III 2994 (26)
12. L&P Vol IV 464 (15)
13. L&P Vol IV 2218

those that supported the new order, particularly the Boleyn family. Catholic sympathisers were only too eager to spread tales that impugned the king and his new wife's name. One such sympathiser, John Hale, the Vicar of Isleworth, claimed when he testified before the king's council that he had *maliciously slandered the King and Queen's Grace and their Council*. Though he initially blamed his slanderous words on his troubled wits and lack of memory at his advanced age, he added that one of his accusers had discussed with him *the king's bodily lusts* and pointed out that young Master Carey was *our sovereign lord, the King's son, by our sovereign lady, the Queen's sister, whom the Queen's Grace might not suffer to be at Court*.[14]

While it may seem as though this is proof of the Carey children's paternity, the words of a man who not only desperately opposed the king, but also admitted that he slandered against him just do not stand up to scrutiny. Among other things, Hale claimed that Henry had *violated most of the women at his court and married Anne Boleyn out of sheer fornication to the highest shame and undoing of himself and all his realm*, and that the king *kept his own brothel of maidens at Farnham Castle*. The vicar was associated with religious leaders at Syon Abbey, who were known to be in support of Catherine of Aragon and would later suffer a traitor's death, hanged and disembowelled at Tyburn, for refusing to acknowledge the royal supremacy and the invalidity of the king's first marriage.[15]

The portraits of the Carey siblings offer additional clues when considering the paternity of Mary Boleyn's children. Around the same time Catherine's portrait was painted by Van der Meulen, an additional portrait was commissioned by her brother. A comparison of the two portraits are a study in contrasts. The small bit of hair escaping from Catherine's coif is the shocking red

---

14. L&P Vol VIII 567
15. Weir, Mary Boleyn pg 155

usually associated with the Tudor offspring, while Henry's hair is a fair brown reminiscent of William Carey.

While Henry's angular features mirror those in Thomas Boleyn's monumental brass, Catherine's face has soft curves and jowls similar to the king. The resemblance between the portrait of Catherine and portraits of Henry VIII and her cousin Elizabeth I are striking, while Henry Carey more closely resembles William Carey and their aunt, Anne Boleyn. It is, however, important to remember that both the Boleyn and Carey families were related to the Tudors and that it is not uncommon for first cousins, like Catherine and Elizabeth, to look more like siblings. Genetics are complex and physical similarities can come in the least expected places. Additionally, recent examinations on the painting have shown some later cosmetic changes and further conservation may reveal that her true facial features are less similar than they appear.

The final piece of circumstantial evidence in the paternity of the Carey children is Catherine's appointment to Anne of Cleves' household upon her arrival at court. A position in the queen's household was highly coveted and very competitive. The fact that Catherine was sought for the position as soon as she came of age speaks volumes. By the time the king reached his fourth marriage, the Boleyn family was all but wiped out of existence. Anne's fall affected her remaining family members and her father, Thomas, never fully regained his favour at court. A majority of the Boleyn lands reverted back to the crown after Thomas's death and any lands that were eligible to be passed on would go to Henry, the last Boleyn heir. Having married a relatively poor soldier, William Stafford, Mary was in no position to advocate for her daughter. It is possible that the Duke of Norfolk, Mary's uncle, arranged for Catherine's appointment, but he was probably far more concerned with the other Howard girl that had also come of age, Katherine Howard and the duke may have been wary of promoting any Boleyn interests after Anne's fall.

HISTORY "In a Nutshell" SERIES

It stands to reason that if the king fathered any of the Carey children the evidence is greatest for Catherine. If he did father Catherine, why then would he not claim her as his own? The king was more than willing to claim his illegitimate son with Bessie Blount, why not his child with Mary?

At the time of Fitzroy's birth, Henry was becoming desperate to claim a male heir. Catherine of Aragon was near the end of her childbearing days and it was around this time that Henry began to question the legitimacy of his marriage. He was eager to show that the fault lay with his first wife and believed he had proved it with the baby boy he was able to conceive with his mistress. An illegitimate female child would never be in a position to inherit the throne and the fact that the king already had a princess would push Catherine's value to him down even more.

Another difference was that Mary was married during the time of her affair with the king. Bessie had been single. The laws of the time stated that any child born to a woman in wedlock belonged to the man she was married to so, biology aside, they lawfully would have been William's Carey's children.

Many historians claim that Henry was notorious for demanding fidelity from his mistresses but Henry was so discreet in carrying them on that it can be hard to find proof demonstrating that was truly the case. However, the lack of children born to Mary and William before and after the affair does seem to point to the truth of this statement. The fact that Mary quickly conceived once she began her relationship with William Stafford also seems to support that Mary only shared her favours with the king. But again, there is no solid evidence to prove that she put marital relations on hold during the affair.

If Mary was sleeping with both the king and her husband, the most likely scenario is that the paternity of Catherine was simply unknown. DNA tests didn't exist in Tudor times and there was no reason for the king to claim a female child that may not have been his. He most certainly would not have been willing to risk his burgeoning relationship with Mary's sister or undermine the legitimacy of any future heirs he would have with her.

Was Catherine the daughter of the king? The limited evidence we have supports either verdict and, until DNA testing is authorised on the remains of the Carey children and Henry VIII, her paternity will remain a mystery.

Early childhood

At the time of Catherine's birth, her father was high in favour and serving the king in the privy chamber. A benefit of the position came in the form of a very well-appointed apartment in the king's lodgings at court. Even though Mary was employed in the queen's service, as a married woman she would have resided with her husband in the king's wing of the castle rather than the queen's. As trusted courtiers, the Careys would have spent most of their time at court, very rarely venturing to the manors they owned, so it is uncertain where Catherine was born.

Mary may have retired to one of the manors in Essex to give birth, but as Alison Weir notes in her biography, there is no record that Mary and William were ever in residence there.[16] Another possibility is that Mary gave birth at court. If Catherine was, in fact, the king's child, she may have been afforded this luxury. The most likely scenario is that Catherine was born at Hever, the Boleyn home in Kent, and spent the first four years of her life in the

---

16. Weir, Mary Boleyn pg 336

HISTORY "In a Nutshell" SERIES

care of the same nannies and tutors who helped raise her mother, aunt and uncle.

A few months into Catherine's fourth year, tragedy struck. A new plague called the sweating sickness was sweeping across the country and on 22 June 1528, her father succumbed to the dreaded illness.[17] The sweat was feared because it was so unpredictable. Everyone was vulnerable no matter age, gender or class. Even though the symptoms were seemingly consistent (fever, headache, pain and profuse sweating), the way they reacted to treatment varied from person to person. One man could drop dead in an instant at the onset of the first symptoms, while another could linger in delirium for up to twenty-four hours. Catherine's aunt and uncle were spared after the disease ran its course through their bodies, but Catherine's father was not as lucky.

Almost immediately upon hearing of William's death, the king wrote to Anne that he had extolled their father to do his duty by Mary to take care of her in her widowhood:

> As touching your sister's matter, I have caused Water Welze to write to my Lord my mind therein, whereby I trust that Eve shall not have power to deceive Adam; for surely, whatsoever is said, it cannot so stand with his honour but that he must needs take her his natural daughter now in her extreme necessity.[18]

Mary's son, Henry, was placed into wardship under the care of Anne while his mother retreated from court and returned to life at Hever. In December, she was awarded a £100 annuity that had previously been paid to her husband from the king.

Mary is not mentioned at court again until October 1532, when she set out in her sister's train on their journey to meet the King of France in Calais, so it would be safe to assume that she spent the

---

17. L&P Vol IV 4408
18. L&P Vol IV 4410

four years after William's death at Hever. It is difficult to know if Mary and Catherine had a close relationship, but it's possible that during this time of grief the two bonded. It was certainly the first time in Catherine's life that she could have been the sole focus of her mother.

Catherine's time at Hever would have been spent like any other child of gentle birth. She would have been raised in the company of servants and tutors in the family home. The Boleyns were known to have a deep respect for intellectual pursuits, so she most likely would have received a well-rounded education that would have included lessons in Latin, classic literature and religion, in addition to music, dancing and needlework. When Mary returned to her sister's service, Catherine may have been able to put these lessons to practical use during short visits to her mother at court.

In the summer of 1533, a heavily pregnant Anne Boleyn was crowned queen. There is no record of Catherine attending this event, but as it was a moment of such grand importance for the Boleyn family, it's possible that Anne's nine-year-old niece was included in the festivities. At some point after this important occasion, Mary left court long enough to become noticeably enceinte by September 1534, when her re-appearance caused enough scandal to have her banished from her sister's service. Where was Catherine during this time?

Several historians have speculated that Catherine was installed in Princess Elizabeth's household some time shortly after her birth. Historians Alison Weir, Elizabeth Norton and Tracy Borman all indicate that this is most likely the case. However, there is no documentation that she was ever at Hatfield. The attendants in the infant princess's household are duly noted and Catherine receives no mention. Additionally, Elizabeth's household was greatly reduced following her mother's fall and any Boleyn influences would have been swiftly removed from Elizabeth's life after Anne's death. Living in such close proximity with the princess would certainly explain the connection that she and Elizabeth shared later in life, but there are other circumstances that could have cemented that bond. It is quite possible that the familiarity between the cousins grew due to the time spent together during Catherine's service to Elizabeth's stepmothers.

It is difficult to trace Mary's whereabouts after her exile from court, but it's unlikely that she returned to Hever. She may have gone to live with the family of her new husband, William Stafford, at their home in Cottered, or she may have followed William to Calais where he served as a spearman to the king's cousin, Viscount Lisle. If Catherine was not serving her cousin at Hatfield, it is possible that she travelled with her mother or she may have remained at Hever.

Courtship and marriage

In Tudor England, more often than not, marriage in the nobility and upper classes was the result of very careful dynastic planning on the part of two families looking to consolidate their interests. It also seems to have been very rare for a courtship to have organically grown between two people out of their own volition. Two people could form affectionate bonds before marriage, but those bonds usually came about because they were already promised to each other or there was an expectation that they would be. It wasn't impossible for two people to fall in love and get married, but it was definitely the exception and not the rule. Sometimes there wasn't even time for a courtship. Marriages could be arranged and consummated in a matter of weeks. Fortunately, there was always a chance that the two strangers who found themselves at the altar would grow to deeply love and respect each other as if they were soulmates.

It is unknown whether the marriage between Francis Knollys and Catherine Carey was the result of a love match or a very lucky arrangement, and the primary documents don't reveal many clues. While there is no clear evidence of Catherine's whereabouts from her birth to around age fifteen, it is documented that Francis sat for parliament before he was appointed to the king's bodyguard in 1539 and, though there is no official record of it, tradition says that he attended Magdalen College, so it is likely that he was around his childhood home of Rotherfield Greys in Oxfordshire for most of his youth.[19] It seems then that the two might have met in November 1539. Both appear in the *Letters and Papers* of Henry VIII. Francis is listed as one of the men sent to greet the king's fourth wife, Anne of Cleves, upon her arrival at Calais and Catherine is listed as one of the maidens ready to meet Anne once she arrived at court.

There aren't any obvious links between the two families, but Catherine's stepfather, William Stafford, is listed in the same welcoming group as Francis. The papers show that Catherine was listed in the group set to meet the queen at Dover, so it is unlikely that they travelled over together if Catherine was living in Calais at the time. She either came over earlier than Francis and her parents or she was already living somewhere in England with her mother. Perhaps William Stafford was so impressed with Francis during their journey together that he instigated a meeting between the two in the hope that they would hit it off. But it can't be ruled out that their marriage was one that was engineered by either the families of Francis and Catherine or by the king.

However Francis and Catherine became a couple, their courtship did not last long. They were married on 26 April 1540 and their first son, Henry, was born less than a year later. The Latin dictionary held in a private collection of a Knollys' descendents can offer some clues into the relationship between husband and wife.

Francis's Latin dictionary is the first volume in a set and contains the letters A to E. Researcher Sally Varlow notes that it was produced in Venice in 1551 and is still in its original calf binding.

---

19. History of Parliament Online

She indicates that Francis most likely picked it up while he was in exile in the Low Countries. The introductory paragraph notes the date of the Knollys' marriage and describes how the writer dated the entries. It goes on to list the names and dates of birth of all fourteen of the Knollys' children.[20]

> Here folowethe in order the names, wt the tymes of the byrthe of the chyldren of Francys Knollys & Katern his wyffe that were maryed ye xxvi daye of Aprylle anno. 1540 & the year of or Lorde is cownted to begyne at kyrstmas.[21]

Varlow's analysis of the handwriting shows that the introductory paragraph and first eleven entries, along with the number twelve, were written at the same time. The twelfth and thirteenth births were recorded together as well in the same hand. The final birth may have been recorded by someone else. When compared to the confirmed handwriting of Francis, the first thirteen entries appear to have been written by him. Since a time of birth is included for the last two births, one could surmise that Francis, himself, was present.[22] While this is not completely out of the ordinary, it does support the idea that Francis and Catherine had a close relationship and he attended at least some of the births when he was able.

Catherine appears to have retreated from court service for the most part during her childbearing years. She is not listed in any records in service to Henry's other queens and as it is known Lettice was born at Rotherfield Greys,[23] one can assume that at least a majority of the other children were born there as well prior to their exile in Germany. Greys had been granted to Francis and Catherine jointly in tail male during the parliament of 1540,[24]

20. Varlow pg 1
21. IBID pg 9
22. IBID pg 2
23. Ford, David Nash Royal Berkshire History
24. L&P XIV C67

and it served as a home-base for the Knollys' family. Francis was continually in service throughout Henry VIII's reign so, judging by the dates of conception for the first five children, Catherine either resided at court in the apartments allotted to Francis or he visited her at their home in Oxford frequently.

In March 1544, Francis appears in the roster of gentleman pensioners who attended the king in his siege against Boulogne.[25] The battle would rage through most of the summer until the French forces surrendered on 13 September 1544. It was the first time during their marriage that Francis participated in military service, but it certainly wouldn't be the last.

In 1547, Henry VIII died and his young son, Edward, came to power. *History of Parliament Online* indicates that Francis took on the position of Master of the Horse for Edward VI[26] that year, but D. E. Hoak lists William Paulet and John Dudley in this position,[27] and the *Calendar of State Papers Domestic: Edward, Mary and Elizabeth* confirms that Herbert was in this position by February 1550. Francis was in service to the new king during the Battle of Pinkie, one of the many skirmishes between England and Scotland during the period known as the Rough Wooing. Francis was knighted on the battlefield at Roxburgh by his commander-in-chief, the Duke of Somerset, on 28 September 1547.[28] Francis continued his varied service to the young king and in November 1552 was in communication with the lord deputy in Ireland.[29]

The death of the Protestant Edward VI and the ascension of his Catholic sister, Mary, in 1553 heralded many changes for the Knollys family, and throughout Mary's reign Francis and Catherine would have found themselves apart far more often. In

---

25. L&P XVIII Pt 1 275
26. History of Parliament Online
27. Hoak pg 368
28. Boase, G.C. Dictionary of National Biography Vol XXXI
29. Cecil Papers Vol I

1557, a pregnant Catherine and five of their children were noted in Frankfurt at the home of London merchant John Weller.[30] The couple remained in Germany until the end of the Marian reign.

The family returned to England upon the ascension of Catherine's cousin, Elizabeth, and both were immediately appointed to positions at court. Catherine was named chief lady of the privy chamber and Francis attained the post of vice chamberlain of the queen's household. It had been some time since husband and wife were both in attendance on the reigning monarch, but the fact that they were both stationed at court did not guarantee that they would spend much time together.

During Elizabeth's reign, Francis spent a fair amount of time traveling on the queen's business. In August 1563, he was dispatched to the garrison at Le Havre to mediate for the council and the troops under the command of the Earl of Warwick.[31] In 1566, the council sent him to Ireland with the intention of ferreting out any wrongdoing by Sir Henry Sidney, the lord deputy, regarding the campaign against the Irish rebels. To Elizabeth's dismay, Francis found nothing out of order and sided with Sidney, approving his plans.[32]

In May 1568, the distraught Mary Queen of Scots fled her home country in search of protection from her royal cousin. It appears that Francis was the one courtier that Elizabeth trusted to handle the delicate situation of imprisoning a queen, and he was sent post-haste to Carlisle Castle. It is a testament to the Knollys' marriage that Elizabeth believed Francis to be the only man who could resist the Scottish queen's seductive charms.

Francis seemed to think that the matter was one that could be quickly resolved, but as the weeks turned into months with no resolution in sight, his letters back to court became increasingly

---

30. Garrett, Survey of the Marian Exiles
31. Cecil Papers Vol 1 898
32. Ford, David Nash Royal Berkshire History

HISTORY "In a Nutshell" SERIES

desperate. He was grasping at anything to get the queen to relieve him of his duty. It is in these final letters that the picture of love and devotion really takes shape.

Carlisle Castle did not afford the protection needed to guard Mary and in July, Francis moved her to Bolton Castle. A few weeks later, Francis wrote to Elizabeth's secretary, William Cecil, of his growing frustration:

> I long to hear from you and therefore "ply" you with letters. We have "extreme need" of money, and I trust soon to be recalled, as my stay here is "superfluous."[33]

He added a note at the end of the letter asking Cecil to give "the enclosed to my wife". Whether the enclosed item was a gift or a letter, we can be sure that even during this trying professional time for Francis, Catherine was on his mind.

Cecil's return letter to Francis must have indicated that Catherine had fallen ill, because only four days after his missive to the secretary, he sent a letter to his wife chiding her for not taking care of herself:

> I am very sorry to hear that you are fallen into a fever. I would to God I were so dispatched hence that I might only attend and care for your good recovery. I trust you shall overcome this fever and recover good health again for although in your health you do often forget to prevent sickness by due and precise order, yet when you are falling into sickness, you will then (although it be late) observe very good order.[34]

---

33. CP Vol 1 739
34. Miscellanies of the Philobiblon Society Vol XIV

While it would be easy to take his chastising as a rebuke, it seems to fall more along the lines of a worried spouse emphasising his concern. He ended the letter:

> Wishing your good and comfortable recovery to your own satisfaction and mine. I shall commend you to God. Your loving husband, F. Knollys.[35]

By the first half of August, Catherine had recovered from the fever she was suffering, but her health continued to be a concern for Francis. Even as Robert Dudley, the master of the horse, responded to the business of getting more horses to the Queen of Scots, he included a note regarding his concern for the wife of his close friend: *I fear her diet and order.*[36]

Catherine's recovery did not last long and Francis's letter to Cecil indicated that their separation was to blame:

> As my wife has lately been sick and moderate travel and quietness of mind are the only means to preserve her health, and she is desirous to come hither if my return be not shortly. I desire you to signify to her by this bearer whether it is likely I shall remain here 5 or 6 weeks longer?[37]

He added that her illness was financially draining him and that it would be prudent for them to be together because it would comfort her spirits. The queen quickly scuttled the plan; Catherine was far too sick to be moved. The news was disappointing to Francis and he extolled the queen to comfort her with *benign clemency and gracious courtesy* in his stead. By the end of the month it was clear that Catherine was suffering from depression: *I pray you comfort my poor wife's disease of the mind, if she have any such dolor.*[38]

---

35. IBID
36. IBID
37. CP Vol 1 772
38. IBID 791

Figure 4 - Detail of the Knollys monument at Rotherfield Greys

Francis's flurry of letters back to court show that he was very concerned for his wife:

The poostes cryed owte on me for vexing theym so often with letters.[39]

It is likely that the man, notorious for speaking earnestly, shared his worries with the woman he was guarding. In September, the Scottish queen made a gift for Catherine, a chain of pomander beads finely laced with gold wire.[40]

In October, Cecil noted in his correspondence to Francis that his wife was feeling better and the fever seemed to abate for the entirety of the month. In a letter on 29 October, Francis asked Cecil to *commend me to my wife, and excuse me not writing to her for haste hereof.*[41] Catherine's health appears to have remained stable throughout November and most of December, but that didn't ease Francis's constant lobbying to be recalled back to court. In almost every letter back to the queen or Cecil he reiterates his desire to return home to the point of rudeness.

The letter to Catherine on 30 December shows Francis's desperation. He had become so angered by the queen's refusal to release him that he almost wrote to her that he did not understand how she could allow his wife to die in such an uncomfortable and miserable state in her own court. He stopped short of sending this accusatory missive when he received word from Cecil that Catherine was feeling better, but his mind was still not eased, even though he felt better having unburdened those thoughts to *you that is another of myself.* It is this phrase that demonstrates more than anything that Francis thought of his wife as an equal.

He told Catherine *to arm yourself against sickness you must make God your refuge and call upon him that these worldly sorrows oppress you not to the hindrance of your health. For God will not leave us.*

---

39. IBID 786
40. IBID 798
41. CP Vol 2 877

HISTORY "In a Nutshell" SERIES

He will provide for us. He raged against the queen saying that even though Catherine had demonstrated great love for her, she still made her weep for unkindness and it had been a detriment to her health. He believed that his trust and her love to the queen had been deemed so unworthy it would be better for them to leave the court and live a poor country life where they could be happy together. He would leave the queen's service if that was what Catherine wished.[42]

Catherine's response to this poignant letter does not survive and only a few short weeks later she succumbed to her illness. Francis stayed with the Queen of Scots until she was safely ensconced at Tutbury, but his grief was so great that his brother, Henry Knollys, had to attend to his matters of business and correspondence with the queen and Cecil.[43] The remaining letters from January paint a picture of a very distressed man. His final letter to the privy council on 29 January states:

> I am much disquieted with this service in these strange countries, which melancholy humor grows daily on me since my wife's death. I am commanded expressly of God that I shall not tempt my Lord my God and my continuance here is intolerable, unless I obey man rather than God. My case is pitiful. For my wife disburdened me of many cares. She kept all the monuments of my public charges as well as my private accounts and now my children, my servants, and all other things are loosely left without good order. But your lordships know all this without my rehearsal and I leave it to your consideration.[44]

---

42. Miscellanies of the Philobiblon Society Vol XIV
43. CP Vol 3 963
44. CP Vol 3 978

Catherine's death seems to have left a large void in Francis's life. He spent the remaining years of his bachelorhood focusing on service to Elizabeth and advocating for his many children. The fact that he lived another twenty-seven years after Catherine's death and never remarried reinforces the idea that, however their marriage came about, it was truly a love match.

Figure 5 - The Knollys monument at Rotherfield Greys

Children

Francis and Catherine wasted no time in building their family. The first of fourteen children was born only a few weeks before their first anniversary. The next ten came with only a year or two between them. Since Francis was serving the king and often away at court, it's likely that, though Catherine isn't listed in service to any other queen than Anne of Cleves, she resided there with him when she wasn't at home birthing the children.

Prior to the discovery of Francis's Latin dictionary in 2006, the number of children that Catherine and Francis had and their names and birth order were up for debate. Their daughter, Lettice, was usually placed first in birth order due to the age recorded on her tomb by the Devereux family, whose history was compiled in 1853. They assumed a birthdate of 1540/41.[45] The simplest explanation for this mistake is that, as a countess twice-over, Lettice would have taken precedence over her brothers and sisters. This could have led later historians to assume she was the eldest. Because of this

---

45. Varlow pg 2

Figure 6 - Portrait of Lettice Knollys c. 1585, Attributed to George Gower (1540-1596) from the Collection of the Marquess of Bath

precedence, her likeness is first in line in the elaborate monument constructed in memory of Francis and Catherine in St Nicholas's Church at Rotherfield Greys.[46] Thanks to Francis's excellent record-keeping skills, it is now certain that Lettice was actually the third child and second daughter.

The monument at Greys and a memorial plaque for Catherine at Westminster Abbey may be the cause for confusion over how many children were in the Knollys family. The Greys monument was erected by their son, William, Earl of Banbury, in 1605 and contains the effigies of Francis and Catherine along with sixteen kneeling figures. On first appearance, the sixteen figures would seem to represent all the Knollys children, but it is more likely that the two figures in ermine robes and coronets on the canopy overhead are William and his wife.[47] There is no date of erection on the plaque on the wall of St Edmund's Chapel in Westminster Abbey, but based upon a Latin inscription, it would be safe to say it was before Francis's death in 1596. It raises the number of children born to the couple to sixteen:

> O, Francis, she who was thy wife, behold, Catherine Knolle lies dead under the chilly marble. I know well that she will never depart from they soul, though dead. Whilst alive she was always loved by thee: living, she bore thee, her husband, sixteen children and was equally female and male (that is, both gentle and valiant). Would that she had lived many years with thee and thy wife was now an old lady. But God desired it not. But he willed that thou, O Catherine, should await thy husband in Heaven.[48]

---

46. IBID
47. IBID
48. Westminster-abbey.org

Figure 7 - Vintage engraving of William Knollys, 1st Earl of Banbury, by Simon van de Passe

It seems most likely that the plaque would be right since it was in place before Francis' death and he would have known how many children were born. However, the Grey's monument was built at the behest of their son, so it would also be right to assume that he would know just as well how many siblings he had. Because of these discrepancies, the Latin dictionary appears to be the most accurate reference. It lists the birth order as follows:

From this listing, we can see that Catherine's pregnancies happened almost in succession with very little time between pregnancies. There appears to be an interval of three years between the birth of the eleventh and twelfth children, which would account for the time that Francis spent in the Low Countries scouting out settlements for the protestant exiles.

In June 1557, Catherine is documented in Germany already two months pregnant with their son, Thomas. We can conclude that Francis was with her during that time period for certain and that the three year break between births most likely means that Catherine did not travel with Francis as had been previously thought, due to the dating of 1553 on the letter sent to Catherine from the future Queen Elizabeth – the *Cor Rotto* letter. One could argue that they were careful not to procreate during their travels, but as Catherine was pregnant during their exile of 1557, that doesn't seem to have been a priority.

Another explanation for the gap between pregnancies, if Catherine was in fact on the continent in 1553, is that the memorials were right in the number of children and two were conceived and miscarried in that time period, but Francis did not document them as they did not live beyond birth. It is possible that children were born and/or miscarried after the last recorded birth, but Catherine was around thirty-eight years old at the time and very close to the end of her childbearing years, so this is less likely. A daughter named Cecilia has often been attributed to the Knollys clan, but most historians now agree that as she does not appear in the Latin dictionary, she most likely did not exist. In a court full of women called Elizabeth or Katherine, there is a high probability that Cecilia or Cecily was used as a nickname for one of the other daughters. As Saint Cecilia is the patron saint of musicians, one of the daughters may have been a particularly good musician or was known to really enjoy music, and that was how the moniker came about. Wherever the name came from, there is no primary source for it in the Knollys family records.

The tradition of the time was to name the first born child after the reigning monarch (if male) or their consort (if female). The first son born to Francis and Catherine follows this tradition. Henry was born around 12 April 1541. He was educated at Magdalen College, close to his home in Oxford, and sat for parliament a number of times. He served Queen Elizabeth during her battle with the Northern Rebels. In 1570, he was appointed esquire of the body. Eight years later, what started out as an interest in setting up in the newly formed North American Colonies turned into more of a privateering venture on the Spanish coast when Henry and the pirate, John Callis, commandeered three of Sir Humphrey Gilberts' ships headed for the New World. Henry was married in 1565 to Margaret Cave in a lavish ceremony held at Durham House and paid for by the queen[49]. They had two daughters, Elizabeth and Lettice.[50]

The first daughter, Mary, was born just before All Hallows Day, around 26 October 1542. Mary was a very common name in Tudor times, but it is possible that she was named for Catherine's mother. If that was the case, it would definitely point to a strong maternal relationship between Catherine and Mary Boleyn. A search in various genealogical records links Mary to a man named Edward Stalker, but there is no primary source to confirm that both Marys were one and the same. Dr Kristin Bundesen, author

---

49. CSP – Spanish 1558-1567
50. History of Parliament Online

of the unpublished thesis *No Other Faction but My Own*, points out that a Knollys daughter shows up in the household accounts of the Duchess of Suffolk for 1560-62.[51] She suggests that this is either Mary or her younger sister, Maude, as daughters Lettice and Elizabeth are already accounted for in Queen Elizabeth's household at this time.

Lettice, the most well-known of the Knollys children, was born on 6 November 1543 and was most likely named in honour of Francis's own mother, also named Lettice. She earned herself the nickname of She-Wolf for her daring flirtation and eventual marriage to the queen's favourite, Robert Dudley, after the death of her first husband, Robert Devereaux, the Earl of Essex. After her banishment from court in the early 1570s, the Countess of Essex and Leicester lived to the ripe old age of ninety-one, outliving her son from her first marriage, Robert Devereaux, who is best known as the queen's last favourite. The untimely death of Robert Dudley, Earl of Leicester, left Lettice a wealthy widow and she followed in the footsteps of her maternal grandmother and married well below her station – Christopher Blount, gentleman of the horse to her dearly departed husband. Lettice's daughters, Penelope and Dorothy, both countesses as well, also had their fair share of marital scandals, while her sons, Francis Devereaux and Robert Dudley, left the world in early childhood.

The second son, William, was born just after Lady Day, around 20 March 1545. William was a common Tudor name, but it is possible that Catherine chose the name to honour her father, William Carey, and/or stepfather, William Stafford. William was the subject of much derision in his cousin's court. His infatuation with his young ward, Mary Fitton, and the layered tri-colour appearance of his beard as he aged became the subject of a taunt that was sang around the court, earning him the nickname of

---

51. Bundesen, pg 137 from the Ancaster Manuscripts. The household accounts of Richard Bertie and Katherine Duchess of Suffolk.

HISTORY "In a Nutshell" SERIES

Party Beard.⁵² The end of Elizabeth's reign brought about his creation as 1ˢᵗ Baron Knollys in 1603, and his star continued to rise under the new monarch, James I, who bestowed upon him the titles of 1ˢᵗ Viscount Wallingford and 1ˢᵗ Earl Banbury⁵³. His first marriage to Dorothy Bray was childless and the two children born to his second wife, Elizabeth Howard, are suspected to be products of her affair with Edward Vaux. After William's death, the House of Lords refused to grant them the Banbury title. In his lifetime, William served as captain in the army of the north, acting governor of Ostend, captain of band of horse, and lord lieutenant of Oxfordshire and Berkshire.⁵⁴

The Latin dictionary notes that Edward was born on Saint Luke's Even, which fell on 18 October 1546, the feast day of that saint. His name likely came from Henry VIII's successor, Edward VI, since their birthdays were so close. Like most of the men in his family, Edward served as a member of parliament. He died in Ireland in 1572, around the age of twenty-six, in the service of his brother-in-law, Walter Devereaux.⁵⁵

Maude was born on 31 March 1548. Before the discovery of the Latin dictionary, she was often confused with her older sister as Maude was an acceptable Tudor nickname for Mary. Maude may have been the daughter listed in the accounts for the Duchess of Suffolk. She would have been over the age of twelve in 1560, certainly old enough to be in service to a noblewoman. However, in a family with such an unusually successful birthrate, the absence of an adult record of her (marriage or death) could be indicative of a childhood death. Since it is uncertain if survival past infancy was required for Francis to have recorded a child's birth, it is unknown whether Maude was alive when her birth was recorded after 1551.

---

52. History of Parliament Online
53. IBID
54. Bundesen, pg 239
55. History of Parliament Online

Elizabeth was born on 15 June 1549, Trinity Sunday. Her flame red hair and pale skin was reminiscent of her royal cousin and it is possible that she was the namesake of the future queen. The fourth daughter of Francis and Catherine was beloved by Queen Elizabeth. She was appointed at the very early age of ten as a maid-of-honour at the beginning of her reign.[56] Elizabeth was married to Thomas Leighton and spent most of her married life at court. Dr Bundesen notes that Thomas was a Marian exile and friend to Francis, and that the advanced age at the time of their marriage indicates that their match may have been one of mutual respect and friendship that developed over their time spent together at court.[57]

Robert was born on 9 November 1550, and was most likely named after Francis's father. He held many titles during his lifetime. In addition to his roles as MP for both Reading and Breconshire, he was the porter of Tower Mint; Keeper of Syon House, keeper of the woods at Iselworth, Brentford, Twickenham, Heston, Whitton, Sutton and Aydestons; steward and bailiff of crown lands at Isleworth; and gentleman of the privy chamber and esquire of the body to Queen Elizabeth.[58] He was held in very high esteem by his royal cousin and her successor, James I. Though Robert was highly respected for his political acumen, he was dogged with debt and many of his goods were seized after his death from a fall he took at his brother William's home. He was married to Catherine Vaughn.

Richard was born on 21 May 1552, and lived a rather unremarkable life. He served as a member of parliament for Wallingford and Northampton and married Joan Heigham. They had three sons and two daughters.

Francis, his father's namesake, was born on 14 August 1553. His date of birth indicates that the later date of 1557 is the most likely year for Catherine's exile to the Low Countries. Catherine

---

56. Bundesen Pg 224
57. IBID pg 117
58. History of Parliament Online

HISTORY "In a Nutshell" SERIES

would have still been recovering from her childbirth when Francis departed in September, and it's very doubtful that she would undertake such a journey during her pregnancy. Francis succeeded his brother, Edward, as MP for Oxford after his untimely death in 1572. He continued to serve as MP several times during his life for Oxford, Berkshire and Reading. Like his older brother, Henry, Francis spent much of his time privateering against the Spaniards and, during the Armada, he was commissioner for musters and colonel of militia in Hertfordshire under his brother-in-law, Robert Dudley, who was serving as lord lieutenant. Francis's daughter was married to John Hampden, one of the leading challengers to the authority of Charles I at the dawn of the English civil war.[59]

Anne was born just before the gap in births on 19 July 1555. She may have been named for Catherine's deceased aunt, the executed queen, Anne Boleyn. However, Anne was a very common name during this time so that may not have been the case. Anne was appointed as a maid of the chamber the same year that Catherine died and likely served the queen until her death.[60] In 1571, she married Thomas West, the son of an attainted traitor. Though Thomas's father was restored to favour under Elizabeth's reign, the title of Baron De La Warre was not returned to the West family until his death in 1595. Anne and Thomas had fourteen children, eleven of whom reached adulthood. Two of their sons, Francis and John, both served as governor in the newly created colony of Virginia.

Second to last son Thomas may have been the only child born during the Knollys' exile. Thomas's birthdate of 26 January 1558, along with the notation of Catherine being in Frankfurt in June 1557, would definitely indicate that she was in the very early stages of pregnancy upon her arrival on the continent. It is unlikely that Catherine would have risked the uncomfortable journey back to

---

59. History of Parliament Online

60. Bundesen pg 114

England while she was with child, and most of the records indicate that Francis and Catherine did not return until early 1559. Thomas seems to have had the same daring nature his elder sister, Lettice, shared. Dr Bundesen relates an incident in 1590 when Thomas and his cousin, Thomas Morgan, abducted the two daughters of Marchioness Maria de Moreda of Dordrecht to save them from arranged marriages to "their enemy", their Spanish Catholic cousins.[61] Thomas's royal cousin declined to take any action against him even though it caused an international incident.

The youngest daughter, Katherine, was born on 21 October 1559. Her birthdate includes the time of day of her birth, indicating that Francis may have been present. Katherine followed her sister into the queen's service in 1575. She was not quite ten at the time of her mother's death, so it is possible that her early years were spent in the care of Lettice. She married Gerald Fitzgerald, Baron Offaly, and their first daughter, Lettice, was named 1st Baroness Offaly. After Fitzgerald's death, Katherine married Sir Phillip Butler.

The last child, a son named Dudley after Francis's close friend, the Earl of Leicester, was born on 9 May 1562. He is the only child of Francis and Catherine who is known definitively to have died shortly after birth. A contemporary record notes that *Sir Francis's childe called Dudley Warwick was killed in June 1562.*[62] The nature of young Dudley's death is unknown and the usage of the word 'killed' does not necessarily indicate foul play. The sad fact of the time period is that many Tudor children did not make it past their first birthday, and it is a matter of astounding odds that so many of the Knollys children made it to adulthood.

---

61. IBID pg 119
62. Archer pg 103

HISTORY "In a Nutshell" SERIES

Figure 8 - Elizabeth Knollys, Lady Leighton, attributed to George Gower, 1577

Catherine at Henry VIII's court

When an opening became available in the crowded court of the reigning monarch, there was often a scramble for the highly coveted positions. Each time Henry found a need to replace his consort's entire household, the leading courtiers rushed to further the careers of the eligible young ladies in their family. Appointment to the queen's household was a privilege and considered a mark of high social standing.[63] The queen's lodgings were separate but identical to those of the king, and made up of four distinct areas: the watching chamber, the presence chamber, the privy chamber and the bedchamber. The higher ranking women served the closest, physically, to the queen in her privy and bedchambers. The lower ranking and younger maids-of-honour tended to be further away from the queen in her watching and presence chambers.

Traditionally, the queen chose her servants, but that was not always the case. Anne of Cleves, a foreign princess with no foreknowledge of the English Court, had her household prepared

---

63. Evans Pg 3

HISTORY "In a Nutshell" SERIES

for her by the king before she set foot on English soil. In addition to being attractive and accomplished at 'womanly skills', other factors were taken into consideration regarding the promotion of an eligible lady including her noble origins, family connections, religious leanings and political influences.[64] In special circumstances, older noble ladies lobbied for the younger girls' appointment, as in the case of the Deputy of Calais, Lord Lisle's stepdaughters. Anne and Catherine Bassett were both put forth as candidates for placement in Queen Jane Seymour's household, but both were initially rejected. Catherine was not as fair as was desired and Anne was deemed too young. At the urgings of Ladies Rutland, Beauchamp and Sussex, Anne was eventually awarded a position as a maid-of-honour once she reached the more acceptable age of sixteen.[65]

A position at court came with a paid wage and, most importantly, room and board. The senior ladies in service were usually married and shared their luxuriously appointed rooms with a spouse who was also serving in the king's household. Since the maids were all unmarried, they received less stately lodgings. They shared a sparse room, with a few beds, that was referred to as the maid's dorm. Each was given a daily allotment of food and drink that could be eaten in the great hall. Only the most favoured servants dined privately with the king and queen.

The duties of the household varied depending upon which rooms the ladies were assigned to. The women of the privy and bedchamber attended to the queen's personal needs. They helped her with a daily hygiene regiment and assisted her as she dressed for the day. The queen rarely slept alone. If the king was not paying a conjugal visit to her bedchamber, her ladies would take turns sleeping on a pallet next to the enormous tester bed. The queen's chamberers took care of menial tasks, making sure that the royal servants kept the lodging clean and freshened. The maids-of-honour

---

64. IBID Pg 10
65. IBID pg 24

were supervised by a Mother of the Maids, and attended the queen publically, carrying her train and providing entertainment.[66] Once a maid was married, she was often promoted to the privy chamber.[67]

Some historians have placed Catherine in service to her aunt, Anne, as she awaited her execution in the Tower of London, but those who waited on Anne were carefully recorded and Catherine is not among these. If Catherine was born in 1524, she would have only been twelve years old at the time of Anne's death, much too young to be in service to the queen unless special accommodations had been made due to their blood relationship.

Wherever it was that Catherine resided from 1534-1539, it is certain that her first foray into court service commenced in November 1539. The first primary evidence for her whereabouts after the fall of the Boleyn family comes from a listing of persons appointed to attend on Henry VIII's fourth wife found in the *Chronicle of Calais*. Note 572 in Volume 14 of Henry VIII's *Letters and Papers* lists the six young ladies designated to meet Anne of Cleves upon her arrival at the English Court. Catherine Carey and her cousin, Katherine Howard, joined Ursula Stourton, Dorothy Braye, Anne Bassett and Mary Norris in their highly coveted position of maids-of-honour to the king's new bride.[68]

It is uncertain whether Catherine came over from Calais with her stepfather, William Stafford, in Anne's train, or if she was already in England at the close of 1539, she may or may not have been witness to the king and his bride's disastrous meeting at Rochester on 1 January. Catherine certainly would have been at the royal palace in Greenwich a few days later participating in the celebrations that preceded the actual wedding.

The arrival of a foreign princess called for great pomp and circumstance. She would need to be properly received into her new

---

66. IBID pg 31
67. IBID pg 32
68. L&P Vol XIV 572

HISTORY "In a Nutshell" SERIES

country to avoid international embarrassment. Preparations would be made to assure that her reception was warm and welcoming, and, most importantly, appropriate for a woman of her status. The *Chronicle of Calais* gives a very detailed and specific list of the men and women that the king requested in anticipation of the arrival of his newest consort.

On 3 January 1540, Anne was officially greeted at Greenwich by the noble ladies who had been appointed by the king to be her closest servants: Margaret Douglas, Eleanor Rutland, Mary Fitzroy, Katherine Brandon, Anne Seymour and Ladies Cheyney, Kingston, Browne, Edgecomb, Baynton, Dudley, Dennys, Knyvett, Wingfield and Heinage.[69] They awaited her at a pavilion in Greenwich Park decorated with cloth of gold and filled with refreshments of wine, fruit and cheese. There she could converse with her ladies, take warmth from the chilly temperature and change her clothing after the journey from Dartford.[70]

After Anne's arrival, Henry processed through the park on horseback accompanied by his trumpeters and privy councillors. He was probably miserable in the knowledge that he would have to proceed with the wedding ceremony even though he was quite repulsed by his new bride.

Catherine was in the nervous group of ladies awaiting their new mistress in the frigid January air. She would not have witnessed the actual wedding ceremony because it was private, but she would have been close to Anne as she eased herself into the English Court. After a two-day rest, Anne's ladies awoke in the early morning light on 6 January to dress her for the nuptials. The actual duty of dressing the queen would have fallen to the higher ranking ladies in service. But Catherine no doubt got to see Anne in her cloth of gold gown, embroidered with delicate pearl flowers and the garland of rosemary branches symbolising remembrance and constancy that

---

69. IBID
70. Warnicke pg 146

entwined her coronal of gold and precious stones atop her loosely worn straw-coloured hair.[71]

After the ceremony, Catherine joined the rest of the queen's ladies in procession to the traditional wedding feast. Once the meal was finished they retreated to the queen's chambers to dress for evening prayers. Customarily, the time between meals would have been spent with entertainment and dancing, but as this wedding took place during Epiphany, they attended Evensong instead. However, like all royal marriage celebrations, the evening culminated in the bedding of the bride. Anne's highest ranking ladies removed all of her finery and assisted her into bed to await the king and the blessing of the priest.[72]

In the weeks that followed, Catherine spent her days in the queen's rooms partaking in the available entertainments. Anne's fondness for cards and gambling would have made it a common pastime in her chambers. The young maids-of-honour would have also worked on their sewing and embroidery with a great deal of time spent on reading or outdoor pursuits, such as archery or horseback riding, all under the supervision of Mother Lowe.[73]

The king's growing distaste for his new wife and Catherine's marriage in April 1540 seem to have prematurely ended her service at court. She may have spent the month of May and the first weeks of June with the queen, but by 24 June, Anne was rusticated to Richmond Palace and Catherine is not among those listed in service. She may have been privy to the whispers around court that the royal marriage had not been consummated. Catherine's aunt, Lady Jane Rochford, was one of the ladies questioned during the divorce proceedings and may have shared her thoughts on the matter with her young niece. Catherine herself seems to have played no role. The notarial record of the divorce signed at

---

71. IBID pg 156
72. IBID pg 159
73. IBID pg 171

HISTORY "In a Nutshell" SERIES

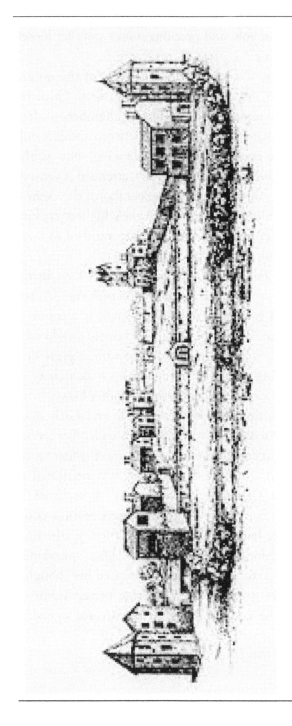

Figure 9 - A vintage etching of Greys Court, courtesy of castles-abbeys.co.uk

Richmond was witnessed by the ladies still in her service: Ladies Rutland, Rochford and Edgecomb, and Dorothy Wingfield, Anne Josselyn and Elizabeth Rastall.[74] By the time the summer heat set in, Catherine would have realised that she was pregnant with her first child. With the chaos swirling around court, Catherine may have found it wise to spend most of her first pregnancy acclimating to her new home at Rotherfield Greys.

The gap of nine months occurring between the birth of Henry and the conception of her second child, Mary, indicates the possibility that Catherine spent some time in service to her newly elevated cousin and queen, Katherine Howard. Having resided together in the dorm as they served Anne of Cleves, a close friendship may have developed between the two and it would not be far-fetched to assume that the new queen made room for Catherine in her household. There are no references to her in Katherine Howard's household, but that may not have been necessary as she was already appointed to the former queen's service. There would be no need to indicate her re-appointment.

Catherine may have accompanied her cousin and the king on their annual progress through England during the summer of 1541, and she may have known about the queen's indiscretions with the king's young groom of the stool, Thomas Culpeper. It appears that Catherine's stepfather, William Stafford, gave evidence against the queen during an investigation throughout the autumn of 1541. The queen's imprisonment at Syon Abbey in November would have marked the end of Catherine's service in her household. It is difficult to say whether Catherine attended the execution of her cousin and her aunt, Lady Rochford, who was implicated in the queen's downfall. It's likely that, finding herself in the early stages of a second pregnancy, Catherine chose to return home to Greys to grieve and spare herself added distress.

---

74. IBID Pg 239

Figure 10 - A modern day photo of Greys Court,
© Dennis Jackson, geograph.co.uk

The absence of a queen between November 1541 and July 1543 allowed Catherine to stay at home and focus on her young family. The third child, Lettice, joined the family in November 1543. The seven months between her birth and the conception of the fourth child, William, and the ten months between William's birth and the conception of the fifth child, Edward, may point to intermittent service to Henry's sixth and final queen, Katherine Parr. However, the gaps in pregnancy could also indicate that Catherine was actually retired from court service at this point, leading to extended periods of separation from her husband. Regardless, Catherine would not have returned to court after the birth of Edward in October 1546. Only three months later Henry VIII died and left his kingdom to his nine-year-old son, Edward.

From the ascension of Edward VI in January 1547 to the ascension of Elizabeth I in November 1558, Catherine was absent from court life. Edward was unmarried so there was no reason to fill the posts of a queen's household. By the time of his death and Mary I's ascension in July 1553, Catherine and her husband were deeply entrenched with the Protestants so the Catholic Mary would not have been interested in recalling her to court. After having loyally served the young king, it appears that Francis Knollys' services were also no longer needed, though he kept his appointment as constable of Wallingford Castle, which he had been awarded for life on 7 March 1551.[75]

The decade following Catherine's release from court service was filled with the births of seven more children and a long, arduous journey across the English Channel to religious exile in the Low Countries.

---

75. Hedges pg 94

HISTORY "In a Nutshell" SERIES

Exile

Catherine and Francis Knollys had successful careers under Henry VIII and his queens and were key players in the Elizabethan court, but they are more well-known for their actions during the reign of Mary Tudor. As Edward VI was taking his last ragged breaths, the protestant faction that had gained momentum under his leadership was busy preparing for their next move. What would they do when the new queen inevitably returned to the Catholic church? The young king tried to head off this calamity by revising the succession document put forth by his father. His intent was to bypass both sisters and name the third in line, Jane Grey, as his successor. His argument was that both sisters had been deemed illegitimate by his father's divorce and annulment. Even though Elizabeth would have kept the religion he preferred, he couldn't very well name Mary a bastard and not hold the same standard for her. By naming the granddaughter of his aunt instead, he could circumvent both of their claims to the throne and promote a protestant.

Edward's plan was ultimately unsuccessful and, after a short skirmish, Mary was proclaimed queen on 19 July 1553. At the outset, Mary adamantly insisted that she had no plans to force anyone to return to the Catholic fold, but it was only a short time before the leading reformists, such as Thomas Cranmer, John Rogers and Hugh Latimer, were imprisoned for heresy. All three would burn at the stake before her reign was over.

There is no indication of Francis's whereabouts during the nine days between Edward's death and Mary's proclamation, and there are no records that include him as part of the protestant coup. He was close to the Dudley family and it is possible that he was in the army of 300 led by Robert Dudley into Norfolk to face Mary, but there is no concrete evidence to prove that and he certainly was not punished for it. The new queen kept on many of her brother's advisors, but Francis was not among them. It is possible that, as a close friend of the Dudleys, he was deemed too radical to keep at court. The esteemed Christina Hallowell Garrett, in her study of the Marian exiles, points out that Francis was certainly known for his religious views by the time of Mary's ascension, having been named as one of the men present on the discussions on the sacrament that took place at both Sir William Cecil's and Sir Richard Morison's homes in 1551.[76]

So where did Francis go after he was dismissed from court? Garrett suggests that Francis was tapped for a very important mission and it is for that reason that Francis initially made his way to the Low Countries, not for fear of persecution. Garrett believed that Francis was sent by Cecil to scout out areas for Protestant settlements and act as an envoy, negotiating an agreement with the Protestant leaders. Cecil's goal was the survival of Protestantism and he realised that he may be required to create a new commonwealth

---

76. Garrett pg 211

to accomplish that. Migration to the continent, where the English could learn to run their own protestant colonies, was the first step.[77]

A letter in the *Catalogue of Lansdowne Manuscripts* in the British Museum has often been used as evidence that Catherine accompanied her husband on this initial voyage out of England. It includes a leaf endorsed in William Cecil's hand *1553 Copy of a letter written by the Lady Elizab; Grace to the Lady Knolles*.[78] It is more commonly referred to as the *Cor Rotto* Letter:

> Relieve your sorrow for your far journey with joy of your short return, and think this pilgrimage rather a proof of your friends, than a leaving of your country. The length of time and distance of place, separates not the love of friends, nor deprives not the show of good will. An old saying, when bale is lowest, boot is nearest; when your need shall be most you shall find my friendship greatest. Let others promise, and I will do, in words not more in deeds as much. My power small, my love as great as them whose gifts may tell their friendship's tale, let will apply all other want, and oft sending take the lieu of often sights. Your messenger shall not return empty, nor yet your desires unaccomplished. Lethe's flood hath here no course, good memory hath greatest stream. And to conclude, a word that hardly I can say, I am driven by need to write, farewell, it is which in one way I wish, the other way I grieve.
>
> Your loving cousin and ready friend,
>
> Cor Rotto

---

77. Garrett pg 7
78. May pg 124

Elizabeth's words give us a pretty clear indication of the affection she felt for her cousin, but it is the dating of the letter that gives pause. A letter from John Calvin to Pierre Viret detailing a visit in Geneva from Francis and his son, Henry, is dated 20 November 1553.[79] Taking into account the amount of time it would take to travel from England to Geneva, Garrett estimates that Francis would have left in September 1553, with either the John à Lasco congregation or the Glastonbury Weavers – less than a month after the birth of their tenth child. It is possible that Francis's fear was so great he would risk his wife and new-born child's health, but it seems more likely that Catherine stayed on at Greys Court with the younger children. Indeed, none of the other Knollys family members are mentioned until much later, when they turn up in Frankfurt Germany in 1557.

William Cecil was a very articulate man and kept excellent records. The fact that the copy was in his possession and dated by him would be evidence enough that it was correctly dated. The most likely explanation is that, in the environment of chaos and fear, misinformation was common. Francis may have initially planned to take Catherine and their family with him, but decided at the last minute that the threat from Queen Mary was not as great as he had anticipated. Perhaps Elizabeth was not informed of the change in plans or the original was never sent. Any number of conclusions can be drawn, but the simplest explanation of all can't be ruled out: Catherine fled with her husband in 1553.

Per the Privy Council Acts of June 1555, Francis was back in England fulfilling his official duties as constable of Wallingford Castle.[80] The birth of his daughter, Anne, the next month puts her conception some time in October 1554. Either Francis's first voyage to the Low Countries was a short one or she was conceived during the journey.

---

79. Garrett pg 211
80. Garrett pg 212

In the winter of 1556, Francis was enrolled at the University of Basle in Switzerland.[81] Catherine's whereabouts during that season are unknown, but she does appear in the home of London merchant John Weller in Frankfurt, Germany, the following summer, on 10 June 1557.[82] She is accompanied by her husband, five of their children, and a maid. It is not certain which children made the journey. The eldest, Henry, would have been sixteen by this time and was likely already pursuing his education at Magdalen College in Oxford. Mary, Lettice, William and Edward were old enough to be serving in the households of the nobility so an argument could be made that they stayed in England. Lettice and Mary may have been in service at Hatfield to Elizabeth. Depending upon whether or not Maude lived into adolescence, the rest of the children may have joined their parents. If Maude was in their number, the youngest, Anne, may have been deemed too young to travel and left at home.

The three-year gap between the birth of Anne and Thomas, the twelfth child, supports the idea that Catherine and Francis did spend some time apart. It is possible that Catherine joined Francis on his second journey to the Low Countries in early 1556, but it is more likely that they reunited in the spring of 1557 in Frankfurt when she conceived Thomas. The burnings of Protestant leaders John Rogers, Laurence Saunders and Rowland Taylor, along with archbishop, Thomas Cranmer, may have been the tipping point that necessitated a family exodus.

Catherine's life in exile would have been very different than what she was used to back home in England. The journey would have been long and difficult. Few exiles chose to travel openly and a train of carts loaded with possessions would have drawn far too much attention. Only the bare necessities were packed for the journey, which would take six weeks at the least. Getting across the

---

81. IBID
82. IBID

English Channel posed its own problems. The sea crossing could be rough and it was reported later to a Mantuan ambassador that at least sixty exiles had been lost to 'fish in the realms of Neptune' on the return trip home.[83]

Accommodations were tight in an already highly populated area and England's elite were forced to take up residence wherever they could. Very often this included living in tight quarters with their servants and other members of the lower classes. Often, more than twenty bodies occupied homes, contributing to a close, crowded environment and a heavily taxed sewer system. This close proximity led to a breakdown in societal structure and the merchant class was able to enjoy an enhanced value that had been denied to them back home.

With an estimated 800 exiles spread out over eight colonies (Emden, Strasbourg, Wesel, Basle, Frankfurt, Aarau, Geneva and Zurich), everyone's vote was deemed important and disagreements erupted on a daily basis. Bickering became a pastime because the exiles often had nothing better to do. The jobs that merchants and artisans traditionally filled in England were full on mainland Europe, and the guilds already established in places like Frankfurt and Strasbourg were hostile to the newcomers who had no interest in learning either the language or customs of their new country. With few social outlets and no employment opportunities, tensions ran high.

In addition to the stresses affecting both genders, women had their own reason for anxiety, childbirth. Garrett notes that there are no official birth records, but based on the census taken of the exiles, it is certain that they did occur.[84] It is highly unlikely that the women were able to bring the midwives they had grown familiar with during their past births, so they had to make do with whoever was available to them when their time came.

---

83. Garrett pg 57
84. IBID pg 53

Thomas Knollys' birth is not recorded in the exile census, but perhaps he was one of the babies born during exile. By the time Catherine shows up in June 1557, in the Weller household, she would have been at least two months pregnant. There is no indication that she returned to England at this point and it is doubtful that she would have commenced such a journey while she was withchild. If she did return before Thomas's birth, neither her husband nor his brother, Henry, accompanied her as both signed the New Discipline adopted by the English church at Frankfurt in December 1557, a mere month before Thomas's birth. This document stated that the congregation was a self-governing body politic, rejecting the jurisdiction of king and bishop.[85]

With all of the tension and chaos plaguing the exile communities, it is safe to say that the day word reached the Low Countries that Queen Mary had died without an heir was one of celebration. Francis and Catherine returned shortly after Mary's death. His admittance on 14 January 1559, as vice chamberlain to Elizabeth's household, was made after most of the other important household promotions.[86] Catherine and her family were witness to the long-awaited coronation of her closest cousin and, within the month, she had conceived her last daughter. Catherine's namesake was their first child born under the rule of the Protestant Elizabeth.

---

85. IBID pg 22
86. IBID pg 212

Figure 11 - A map of Frankfurt in 1572

Catherine and Henry

Separation of the two Carey siblings would come within the first two years of their father William Carey's death. In Tudor society, the lands belonging to a child heir were often awarded in lucrative wardships to the king's favourites. The idea was that the custodian would purchase the wardship from the king and run the lands, using income derived to care for the child until he or she reached their majority. In return, the custodian would, of course, be entitled to some of those rents. The value of Henry's wardship was around £133 6s. 8d.[87] Wardships were not always granted to family members, but in Henry's case it was. At some point after June 1528, Henry joined the royal court as a ward of his aunt.[88]

Anne was a judicious custodian and offered Henry many educational opportunities that would have otherwise been unavailable to him had his aunt not been the king's mistress and intended bride. In addition to time spent studying at a Cistercian

---

87. History of Parliament Online
88. Hart pg 61

monastery, he came under the tutelage of Nicholas Bourbon, a French poet who Anne favoured.[89] When he wasn't in the care of his tutors, Henry spent his days learning courtly skills in the royal household and fraternising with the king's son, Henry Fitzroy. Catherine's location during Henry's wardship under Anne is unclear, but it is inconceivable that any relationship between the two was allowed to flourish during this period. Catherine may very well have visited the court intermittently during her aunt's reign, but her stays would have been short and only the briefest of reunions would have been possible. It wasn't until Anne's fall from grace that brother and sister would have the opportunity to forge a connection.

Henry disappears from the court records until his marriage to Anne Morgan in 1545, when he was noted to be 'of the King's Household'.[90] However, some historians have argued that he was actually in Princess Elizabeth's household at Hundson during this time. The fact that Henry was named Baron Hunsdon would certainly support the argument. Henry may have spent his remaining minority in the princess's household, yet it is possible that Henry was returned to the care of the Boleyn family after his aunt's execution. Tradition has often placed Catherine in the princess's household as well, so it is possible that they were reunited for a few years at either Hever or Hunsdon before Catherine was summoned to court in November 1539.

This extended separation of brother and sister may seem strange to the twenty-first century perspective, but during the sixteenth century it was far more prevalent. Once children entered their prepubescent years, it was quite common for siblings to be sent into different noble houscholds for educational purposes. Girls would be sent off to learn vital skills for their future marriages and hopeful court appointments, and boys would be sent to learn

---

89. IBID
90. History of Parliament Online

how to efficiently run their estates or enter a public profession. Additionally, as in the case of the Boleyn children, siblings could be sent to different countries to learn in foreign courts. Mary and Anne Boleyn both spent significant amounts of time on the European continent far away from their younger brother, George.

Henry and Catherine may have spent some time together throughout the rest of Henry VIII's reign, but once Francis and Catherine began building their family, the opportunities for the siblings to be together at court would have been few and far between. While Catherine was giving birth and possibly serving Henry's final queen, Henry was accepting his first military orders under the command of Viscount Lisle, first at Portsmouth and then as a member of his embassy to France.[91]

Once Henry entered his majority, he spent much of his time at his lands in Buckinghamshire, where he became a member of parliament. The unmarried Edward VI was on the throne, so there was no reason for Catherine to be at court and, when Henry wasn't running his estates, he was out of the country on the king's business. Under Mary's reign, the separation continued. While Catherine and her husband were furthering the Protestant effort, Henry was appointed to a position in either Mary or Elizabeth's household as carver of the privy chamber, and in 1553 was sent abroad to visit the Duke of Savoy to determine his suitability as a husband for Princess Elizabeth.[92]

It really wasn't until Elizabeth's ascension in 1558 that Henry and Catherine were reunited in any permanent way. Once their royal cousin inherited the throne, both were appointed to substantial household positions that kept them in close proximity. A few years after Henry's noble creation as Baron Hunsdon, he was appointed as captain of the gentlemen pensioners and effectively

---

91. IBID
92. IBID

became the queen's personal bodyguard.⁹³ For the next four years, Catherine and Henry worked side-by-side until Henry was appointed Governor of Berwick, where he spent the last months of Catherine's life.

Henry was known to have been aloof and rather rough in speech. He wasn't overly friendly and certainly wasn't charming. Yet he seems to have made an exception when it came to family. Henry's first son, George, was likely named in honour of his deceased uncle, and his first daughter bears the same name as his sister. Several times he refers to Catherine's husband as his brother, and he eventually sends George to Bolton to assist Francis in his dealings with the Queen of Scots.⁹⁴ Throughout Francis's time at Bolton, he appears to have written to Henry just as much as he wrote to his wife. One letter to her ends with this missive:

> *I praye youe remember me to my brother, with thanks also for his letter desiryng hym to pardon my not wrytyng presently to hym, synce I am otherwaies tyred with wrytyng in this unthankfull service.*⁹⁵

Their relationship was close enough that Francis, very boldly, suggested his nephew as a suitable husband for the Scottish queen at the risk of his own queen's wrath.⁹⁶

While sources depicting the relationship between the siblings is almost non-existent, there are extensive references to the queen's adoration for her cousins. This would suggest a close family bond that included all three of them. Dr Bundesen notes that Robert Dudley often referred to the Carey cousins as the biblical tribe of Dan. This remark is particularly illustrative of their close

93. Dictionary of National Biography
94. CSP Foreign Elizabeth Vol VIII 2496
95. Miscellanies of the Philobiblon Society Vol XIV – Francis also had a brother named Henry, but in this letter it is thought that he is referring to Catherine's brother.
96. CSP Foreign Elizabeth Vol VIII 2626

relationship due to the fact that Elizabeth represented herself as the prophet Daniel during her coronation entry into London.[97]

The steady separation of the two siblings over the years would certainly make it difficult for the two to form a close familial bond, but it wouldn't make it impossible. Anne and George Boleyn were known for their deep friendship and they spent most of their childhood apart. The lack of reference to their personal relationship also doesn't mean it never existed. The private moments of everyday life were rarely recorded and it is possible that, having lost so many family members so early in their lives, they were drawn together in their shared grief in the short bursts of time they were together.

---

97. Bundesen pg 75

Figure 12 - Portrait of Henry Carey (Catherine's brother), 1st Baron Hunsdon by Steven van Herwijck c. 1561-1563

Catherine at Elizabeth I's court

The death of Mary I on 17 November 1558 heralded the end of the Catholic majority at court. By Elizabeth I's coronation on 15 January 1559, most of the exiled Protestants had returned to take up the coveted positions denied to them under the previous queen. Catherine's close familial relationship to her Boleyn cousin all but guaranteed an appointment to the new monarch's household. In fact, the *Cor Rotto* letter sent from Elizabeth to Catherine upon her departure to the Low Countries falls just short of promising it.

True to Elizabeth's word, both Francis and Catherine received lucrative positions immediately upon their return from Germany. Catherine was appointed chief lady of the privy chamber and Francis was named vice chamberlain and appointed to the privy council. Coveted positions in the household were also given to daughters Lettice and Elizabeth Knollys.

In addition, Catherine was appointed keeper of the queen's jewels, and one of her earliest duties was to assume custody and take account of the royal jewels from Lady Jane, Countess de Feria,

HISTORY "In a Nutshell" SERIES

with Mrs Norris and Mrs Blanche Parry.[98] In addition, she was responsible for the various gifts Elizabeth received – one being a chained monkey.[99] In the summer of 1565, after the death of Katherine Ashley, former childhood governess of Elizabeth, Catherine was promoted to the position of chief lady of the bedchamber.

As Elizabeth was a reigning queen and not just a consort, she required a much larger household. In her private chambers alone she was served by seven ladies of the bedchamber, six maids-of-honour and four chamberers. In addition to the duties they performed under her predecessors, Elizabeth's ladies studied the bible and read aloud classic works to their mistress. They also performed specialised tasks – one woman's sole job was to scatter fresh flower petals in the queen's path. [100]

The early years of Elizabeth's reign marked several grants to the Knollys family: keepership of Syon Abbey, manors at Taunton and Somerset and various other leases. In 1563, Francis was appointed Captain of Portsmouth and was sent to supervise the dispatch of supplies to the defenders of Le Havre. After he advised a retreat, he headed to the Channel Islands and the Isle of Wight to inspect the queen's defences there.[101] The queen showed great appreciation for her Knollys kin by sponsoring their eldest son Henry's wedding to Margaret Cave. The match itself was a promising one. Margaret was the daughter of Ambrose Cave, the chancellor of the Duchy of Lancaster and a member of Elizabeth's privy council. However, the queen went one step further and paid for a significant portion of the ceremonial festivities.

Catherine's position at court kept her in close personal contact with the queen. Her promotion to the bedchamber required her to

---

98. CSP Undated 1559 Vol VIII 24
99. Borman, Pg 291
100. Weir, Life of Elizabeth pg 258
101. History of Parliament Online

spend alternating nights sleeping on a pallet next to the royal bed. She most likely served well into the later months of her last two pregnancies. Elizabeth was very possessive of her ladies and did not like to be parted from them until absolutely necessary.[102] She would have been expected back at court as quickly as possible after the birth of her children.[103] Catherine would have joined the queen, along with eight other women, as she privately dined. She would also have been among the ladies who prepared the queen for the day, dressing her in the elaborate gowns and ruffs that Elizabeth was known for and applying the fine white powder Elizabeth used on her face to keep herself looking youthful.

Catherine's intimate relationship with the queen would be remarked upon throughout her service. It was often said that she was 'in favour with our noble queen, above the common sort'.[104] But that special relationship often came at a hefty price. As the queen's beloved cousin, Catherine was needed in constant attendance. Visits home to see her children were often out of the question. In addition, Elizabeth often subjected her closest servants to emotional outbursts when she felt as though they had slighted her in some way. She was even known to slap her ladies for minor offences.[105] Francis mentions Elizabeth berating Catherine to tears in his final letter at the end of her life. This was probably exacerbated by the fact that he expected Catherine to serve as an intermediary when he disagreed with the queen's policies, placing added stress on the relationship. The Knollys family was richly rewarded for their loyalty and service to Elizabeth, but the favoured position came with many drawbacks.

The end of Catherine's life was probably a very lonely and stressful time. The separation from Francis and her children and the

---

102. Merton pg 57
103. IBID pg 59
104. Borman Pg 291
105. Weir, Life of Elizabeth pg 258

rigors of her position in the bedchamber may have pushed a minor illness into one that was life-threatening. Regardless of the cause of her early demise, Catherine's death was an intense time of grief for the woman she faithfully served. It is hard to say if Elizabeth ever fully recovered from the death of her close confidante, servant and friend.

Death

The pressures of serving a demanding queen from a position of favour and the depression Catherine suffered due to the absence of her beloved husband seem to have taken their toll during the latter part 1568. By the end of July, she was taken ill with a fever that would plague her intermittently over the next seven months.[106]

A letter dated 9 August 1568 from Robert Dudley to Francis would lead us to believe that, though the initial fever passed rather quickly, Catherine's illness was still taken very seriously. Dudley warned Francis that his wife was not taking proper care of herself and he that feared for her health. His specific words indicate a poor diet.[107] He may have been referring to a propensity for eating the wrong foods. The Tudors were notorious for their fear of fresh fruits and often believed that the eater could assimilate characteristics of the food they were consuming.[108] Or, perhaps, the opposite was

---

106. Miscellanies of the Philobiblon Society Vol XIV
107. IBID
108. Albala pg 167

HISTORY "In a Nutshell" SERIES

true and she was not getting enough nutritional sustenance. The physical effects of depression were not widely recognised at that time, but it is now recognised that a lack of appetite is one of the hallmarks of the condition.

A few weeks later, Francis's letter to Cecil notes that his wife has 'lately been sick'.[109] It would seem that he was referring to the fever that Catherine suffered in July and not a second bout, but only a few days later he notes in a follow-up correspondence that the queen had refused to allow her to travel to Bolton, lest it make her worse.[110] It is possible that Catherine never did fully recover from her initial fever. Francis was very discomfited by his wife's poor state, but the queen needed him to do his job. It was a matter of national security. Perhaps both Dudley and Cecil felt that it was in Francis's best interest that he not be made aware of just how sick Catherine was. Though life expectancy in the Tudor age was much shorter than today, Catherine, in her early forties, was still relatively young and there does not seem to have been any outbreak of plague or sweating sickness at the time she fell ill. It is quite possible that, even though they took her fever seriously, they never really believed that it was life-threatening.

At the end of August, Francis asked Cecil to comfort his wife's 'disease of the mynde'.[111] Catherine's fever had abated for the meantime, but her depression, as well as his, was deepening the more time they spent apart. The biological connections of the body and mind were not understood as well back then as they are today and, based upon twenty-first-century medical research, it could be surmised that Catherine had significant ailments. Chronic pain, gastrointestinal problems, exhaustion and sleep deprivation are all linked to severe depression. In fact, the worse the depression,

---

109. C.P. Vol I 772
110. IBID 786
111. IBID 791

the more severe the physical symptoms are and, unfortunately, the pain often increases the duration of the depression.[112]

In October, Catherine seemed to have been well-amended. Cecil assures Francis of her *healthie estate*[113] and his correspondence back to court takes on a more business-like tone. After the impassioned letter to Cecil in September, in which Francis rages about his ill-treatment and threatens to leave the queen's service,[114] his letters from October and November are far more sedate. He was still irritated at the queen's refusal to let him return home, but he was resigned to do his duty.[115]

At some point after Francis's letter to Cecil on 19 November, and before his final letter to Catherine on 30 December, she again took ill. The emotional distress demonstrated in Francis's letter shows the severity of her sickness. He blamed Catherine's troubles on the queen's mistreatment and *commended her to God as He would comfort her*.[116] His letter to Cecil two weeks later thanks the secretary for comforting his wife in her 'sycklye and dolfull estate'.[117] It was sent on 13 January 1569. Two days later, on 15 January, Catherine succumbed to her illness.

Catherine's death was deeply grieved, not only by her immediate family but also by Queen Elizabeth, the woman she dutifully served for a decade. Elizabeth was distraught by her cousin's sudden passing. Her doleful state was remarked upon by many of her visitors and she used her own funds to pay for an elaborate – almost royal – funeral at Westminster. The payments by warrant of the privy seal for the year running from 20 July 1568

---

112. Madhukar H. Trivedi M.D.
113. C.P. Vol II 849
114. IBID 811
115. IBID 880, 883, 887, 891
116. Miscellanies of the Philobiblon Society Vol XIV
117. C.P. Vol III 948

Figure 13 - The Westminster monument of Catherine Knollys
© 2015 Dean and Chapter of Westminster

Death

to 9 July 1569 list a payment of £640. 2s. 11d. for her burial.[118] The hearse that carried her to her final resting place was richly designed and coveted by the Dean of Westminster and the heralds.[119]

Catherine's resting place is marked by an alabaster monument in the Chapel of St Edmund. The inscription reads:

> The Right Honorable Lady Katherin Knollys Cheeffe Lady of the Quenes Maties [Majesty's] Beddechamber and wiffe to Sr. Frances Knollys Knight Tresorer [Treasurer] of her Highnes Howsholde. Departed this lyefe the 15. of January 1568. At Hampton Courte. And was honorably buried in the flower [floor] of this chappell. This Lady Knollys and the Lord Hundesdon her brother were the childeren of William Caree Esquyer, and of the Lady Mary his wiffe one of the doughters and heires to Thomas Bulleyne Erle of Wylshier [Wiltshire] and Ormond. Which Lady Mary was sister to Anne Quene of England wiffe to Kinge Henry the Eyght father and mother to Elizabeth Quene of England".

Underneath, a Latin inscription says:

---

118. Cecil Papers Vol I 1314
119. Bundesen pg 103

> O, Francis, she who was thy wife, behold,
> Catherine Knolles lies dead under the chilly
> marble. I know well that she will never depart
> from thy soul, though dead. Whilst alive she was
> always loved by thee: living, she bore thee, her
> husband, sixteen children and was equally female
> and male (that is, both gentle and valiant). Would
> that she had lived many years with thee and thy
> wife was now an old lady. But God desired it not.
> But he willed that thou, O Catherine, should
> await thy husband in Heaven.[120]

We may never know exactly what malady overcame Catherine in the final months of her life, but it can be said with great certainty that her passing was a severe blow to those who knew her. Devastated by his wife's untimely passing, Francis never remarried and lived out his remaining twenty-seven years as a bachelor. Elizabeth was said to be inconsolable and took special care to look after the Knollys family. Catherine's legacy lives on in the descendants of her fourteen children, one of whom occupies the British throne today.

---

120. Westminster-abbey.org

Acknowledgements

I would like to thank Dr Kristin Bundesen for graciously directing me to her unpublished thesis after she happened upon an article I authored on the Knollys children for my *Cor Rotto: A Novel of Catherine Carey* blog tour. I had been previously unaware of its existence and found it to be filled with excellent information on the relationships Elizabeth shared with her Carey cousins. Dr Bundesen's analysis was very insightful and I greatly appreciate the information she shared with me regarding Catherine's children. I highly recommend this work for a more in-depth analysis on the politics of serving in Elizabeth's court.

I would also like to thank authors Claire Ridgway and Wendy J. Dunn for all of their encouragement and support.

References

Primary Sources

Calendar of the Cecil Papers in Hatfield House, Vol 1 1306-1571, Her Majestie's Stationary Office, London *(1883)*

Calendar of State Papers Domestic Series of the Reign of Edward VI 1547-1553, Knighton, C. S. (ed) (1992).

Calendar of State Papers Domestic Series, Elizabeth, Vols 1-8 with Addenda, Green, M. A. E., Lemon R., Crosby A. J. and Stevenson, J. (eds) (1865-71)

Calendar of State Papers Scotland, Vols I and II 1547-1569, Bain, Joseph (ed) (1898-1900)

Calendar of State Papers Spain, 13 Vols 1485-1558, de Gayangos, Pascual (ed) (1862-1932)

Household Expenses of the Princess Elizabeth During her Residence at Hatfield October 1, 1551 to September 30, 1552, Strangeford, Viscount (ed) (1853)

Letters and Papers Foreign and Domestic of the Reign of Henry VIII, vols I-XXI, Brewer, J., J. Gardiner and R. H. Brodie (eds) (1876-1932)

Philobiblion Society Miscellanies, vol XIV,Papers relating to Mary, Queen of Scots, Mostly Addressed to or Written by Sir Francis Knollys (1872)

The Lisle Letters, 5 Vols, St. Clair Byrne, M. (ed) (1981)

Secondary Sources

Albala, Ken. *Eating Right in the Renaissance,* University of California Press, Berkeley, 2002.

Archer, Ian W. *Religion, Politics, and Society in Sixteenth-Century England,* Royal Historical Society, Cambridge, 2003.

Boase, G. C. *Dictionary of National Biography* Vol XXXI.

Borman, Tracy. *Elizabeth's Women,* Bantam Books, New York, 2009.

Bryson, Sarah. *Mary Boleyn in a Nutshell,* MadeGlobal, Almeria Spain, 2015.

Evans, Victoria Sylvia. *Ladies-in-Waiting: Women Who Served at the Tudor Court,* ebook, 2014.

Garrett, C. H. *The Marian Exiles,* Cambridge University Press, 1966.

Hart, Kelly. *The Mistresses of Henry VIII,* The History Press, Gloucestershire, 2009.

Hedges, John Kirby. *The History of Wallingford Vol II,* William Clowes & Son Limited, London, 1881.

Hoak, D. E. *The King's Council in the Reign of Edward VI,* Cambridge University Press, 1976.

May, Steven W. ed. *Queen Elizabeth I: Selected Works,* First Washington Square Press, New York, 2005.

Norton, Elizabeth. *The Boleyn Women,* Amberley Publishing, Gloucestershire, 2009.

Porter, Linda. *Katherine the Queen: The Remarkable Life of Katherine Parr.* Macmillan, 2010.
Ridgway, Claire. *Sweating Sickness in a Nutshell,* MadeGlobal, Almeria Spain, 2014.
Ridgway, Claire. *The Anne Boleyn Collection,* MadeGlobal, Almeria Spain, 2012.
Somerset, Anne. *Elizabeth I,* St. Martin's Press, New York, 1991.
Starkey, David. *Elizabeth: The Struggle for the Throne,* HarperCollins Publishers, New York, 2001.
Varlow, Sally (August 2007) *Sir Francis Knollys' Latin Dictionary: New Evidence for Katherine Carey.*
Warnicke, Retha M. *The Marrying of Anne of Cleves.* Cambridge University Press, 2000.
Weir, Alison. *Mary Boleyn the Mistress of Kings,* Ballantine Books, New York, 2011.
Weir, Alison. *The Life of Elizabeth I,* Ballantine Books, New York, 1998.
Wilkinson, Josephine. *Mary Boleyn: The True Story of Henry VIII's Favourite Mistress,* Amberley Publishing, Gloucestershire, 2010.
Westminster-Abbey.org

Unpublished PhD Thesis

Bundesen, Kristin, *"No Other Faction but My Own:" Dynastic Politics and Elizabeth I's Carey Cousins,* University of Nottingham, 2008
Merton, C. *"The Women who served Queen Mary and Queen Elizabeth: Ladies, gentlewomen and maids of the privy chamber, 1553-1603",* Trinity College, Oxford,1992.

Online Resources

David, Jessica. "Conservation Examination Reveals Lady Knollys's Past," 2015 http://britishart.yale.edu/featured-story/53/1863
Ford, David Nash *Royal Berkshire History.*
http://www.berkshirehistory.com/bios/fknollys.html
History of Parliament Online
The History of Parliament: the House of Commons 1509-1558, ed. S.T. Bindoff, 1982
http://www.historyofparliamentonline.org/volume/1509-1558/member/carey-henry-1526-96
http://www.historyofparliamentonline.org/volume/1558-1603/member/knollys-sir-francis-1512-96
Madhukar, H. Trivedi M. D. The Link between Depression and Physical Symptoms, 2004
www.ncbi.nlm.nih.gov/pmc/articles/PMC486942/ Accessed 06/04/2015.
The Dean and Chapter of Westminster.
'Katherine Knollys,' 2013
http://www.westminster-abbey.org/our-history/people/katherine-knollys.

HISTORY "In a Nutshell" SERIES

Illustrations

Figure 1 - Portrait of a woman,
probably Catherine Carey, Lady Knollys
by Steven van der Meulen, 1562.................. 4

Figure 2 - William Carey
attrib. Hans Holbein the Younger, circa 1528.................. 10

Figure 3 - Portrait of Sir Francis Knollys, artist unknown.................. 12

Figure 4 - Detail of the Knollys monument at Rotherfield Greys..... 30

Figure 5 - The Knollys monument at Rotherfield Greys.................. 34

Figure 6 - Portrait of Lettice Knollys c. 1585,
Attributed to George Gower (1540-1596) from the
Collection of the Marquess of Bath.................. 36

Figure 7 - Vintage engraving of William Knollys,
1st Earl of Banbury, by Simon van de Passe.................. 38

Figure 8 - Elizabeth Knollys, Lady Leighton,
attributed to George Gower, 1577.................. 46

Figure 9 - A vintage etching of Greys Court,
courtesy of castles-abbeys.co.uk.................. 52

Figure 10 - A modern day photo of Greys Court,
© Dennis Jackson, geograph.co.uk.................. 54

Figure 11 - A map of Frankfurt in 1572.................. 64

Figure 12 - Portrait of Henry Carey (Catherine's brother),
1st Baron Hunsdon
by Steven van Herwijck c. 1561-1563.................. 70

Figure 13 - The Westminster monument of Catherine Knollys
© 2015 Dean and Chapter of Westminster.................. 78

Other books in this series:

ISBN: 978-15-009962-2-2

In **Sweating Sickness in a Nutshell**, Claire Ridgway examines what the historical sources say about the five epidemics of the mystery disease which hit England between 1485 and 1551, and considers the symptoms, who it affected, the treatments, theories regarding its cause and why it only affected English people.

In **Mary Boleyn in a Nutshell**, Sarah Bryson discusses the controversies surrounding Mary Boleyn's birth, her alleged relationships with two kings, her portraiture and appearance, and her life and death. Mary survived the brutal events of 1536 and was able to make her own choices, defying the social rules of her times by marrying for love. It is from Mary that the Boleyn bloodline extends to the present day.

In **Thomas Cranmer in a Nutshell**, **Beth von Staats** discusses the fascinating life of **Thomas Cranmer**, from his early education, through his appointment to Archbishop of Canterbury, his growth in confidence as a reformer, the writing of two versions of the English Book of Common Prayer and eventually to his imprisonment, recantations and execution.

In **Henry VIII's Health in a Nutshell**, Kyra Kramer highlights the various health issues that Henry suffered throughout his life. Theories for the causes of these problems are discussed, and many "facts" which are accepted as true are challenged.

Freelance medical anthropologist, **Kyra Kramer**, author of *"Blood will Tell"* combines her own research into Henry VIII with theories on his health from other historians through the ages.

ABOUT THE AUTHOR

Adrienne Dillard, author of "*Cor Rotto: A Novel of Catherine Carey*" and "*Catherine Carey in a Nutshell*" is a graduate with a Bachelor of Arts in Liberal Studies with emphasis in History from Montana State University-Northern.

Adrienne has been an eager student of history for most of her life and has completed in-depth research on the American Revolutionary War time period in American History and the history and sinking of the Titanic. Her senior university capstone paper was on the discrepancies in passenger lists on the ill-fated liner and Adrienne was able to work with Philip Hind of Encyclopedia Titanica for much of her research on that subject.

MadeGlobal Publishing

Non Fiction History

- Jasper Tudor - **Debra Bayani**
- Tudor Places of Great Britain - **Claire Ridgway**
- Illustrated Kings and Queens of England - **Claire Ridgway**
- A History of the English Monarchy - **Gareth Russell**
- The Fall of Anne Boleyn - **Claire Ridgway**
- George Boleyn: Tudor Poet, Courtier & Diplomat - **Ridgway & Cherry**
- The Anne Boleyn Collection - **Claire Ridgway**
- The Anne Boleyn Collection II - **Claire Ridgway**
- Two Gentleman Poets at the Court of Henry VIII - **Edmond Bapst**
- A Mountain Road - **Douglas Weddell Thompson**

"History in a Nutshell Series"

- Sweating Sickness in a Nutshell - **Claire Ridgway**
- Mary Boleyn in a Nutshell - **Sarah Bryson**
- Thomas Cranmer in a Nutshell - **Beth von Staats**
- Henry VIII's Health in a Nutshell - **Kyra Kramer**
- Catherine Carey in a Nutshell - **Adrienne Dillard**

Historical Fiction

- Between Two Kings: A Novel of Anne Boleyn - **Olga Lyakina**
- Phoenix Rising - **Hunter S. Jones**
- Cor Rotto - **Adrienne Dillard**
- The Claimant - **Simon Anderson**
- The Truth of the Line - **Melanie V. Taylor**

PLEASE LEAVE A REVIEW

If you enjoyed this book, *please* leave a review at the book seller where you purchased it. There is no better way to thank the author and it really does make a huge difference! *Thank you in advance.*

Lightning Source UK Ltd.
Milton Keynes UK
UKOW06f1237261115

263511UK00011B/204/P